A BALISTRERI COLLECTION

abc poems · maggie balistreri

ISBN-13: 978-0-61577498-5
ISBN-10: 0615774989

Cover design by Efrat Yardeni

Published by
The Em Dash Group
New York NY

In these 26-word ABC poems, or abecedarians, the first word starts with A, the second with B, and so on through the alphabet.

Contents

QUEER RUSES

Are babies crying? Does
every family grate?
Heave it. Jettison
kin; loosen malice's noose.
Old Pop's queer ruses
strangle. This unchurched
vagrant world
x-actoes your zeal.

TWO-STEP

1. A bit closer, dear
   every frantic
   grip, hip instinctively juts
   kitten love made nasty
   Oh, press quietly
   ravel sensuality
   trigger unlapped vigor
   wail x-rated

2. Yank zippers.

maggie balistreri

LANGUOR

Argosy boats chug down estuaries.
Filmy grime hunkers indecently.
Japing kites loom, menacing,
nearing overhead.
Passersby queue 'round
safety tape. Unfurled
veils wave. Xebecs yaw, zig-
zagging.

RED-LIGHT DISTRICT

Alluring blonde
courtesan district
enticing flash
garish haberdashery.

Investigate jalousie's keyhole:
Lascivious merchant
Neon offer promises
quote,
Relaxation/Stimulation Therapy,
unquote.
Visit warily. X-rated yayas zone.

TRIBE UNWILLING

A bus careers
down East Fourteenth.
Gray-haired indigent junkies
kick legs (meth numbed).
Open palms quiz
reluctant samaritans—tribe unwilling.
Vamping winos, x-rated.
Years zoom.

XENOBRETHREN

A bookstore clerk dreads each
Friday's geriatric:
heebeejeebee-inducer,
joints kinked lips moist natty outfit
pressed. Questions
repeated. Straining
to understand.
Vague whimper.
Xenobrethren
yesteryear's Zeus.

AND THEY'RE OFF

a blue corvette
       driver's ed
              first go

hits ignition   jets kick

       lowriders manage nice!
offroad prowls, quayside
racing strips' tartop unfurls

vanishing wheels
x-er youth zoomed

BRA GAGA

A bosom-clenching deftness
enlarging fronts, grunts, heaves

inducing jeering, kid leering
mammary nests
ogling pests quaver
randy shadies tempt unkempt vice
Woven xes yoke ziggurats.

HE-MAN

Another boy charmer
dick engorger, fly-grabbing honey
instigating joy. Killer lips
mouthing nasty overtures.
Pussy Queen rest-stop trollops
       undulating vamps
weaken

x-rated youth zone

HABIT'S INCISORS

After breakfast conversation
died. Each feels grim
habit's incisors—jagged
knives—lockjaw mouths. Neither
occasions passion. Quasiconscious
reticence saps
talk. Untapped
vows. Xeroxed
yawns.
ZZZZZ.

YELLOW ZEROS

Aptly blooded, carnivores
devour entire flanks
gristled haunches included.
jerk kabobs lapping marrow
nibbling orifices.
Philistine quintessence
rapacious slobs target unctuous victuals
wannabe Xerxes
yellow zeros

SLOWLY BUT SURELY

Altricial birds caw
  desperate entreaties form
gradually hovering intermundane
journey kinward
learning ma's nest osmotically
powerless quills rustle
shake tentatively
unfurl
       voilà!

             Waving xes

yearlings zoom

SIMIAN TWINS

Apes bang cage doors enraged.

Forgive God his irreverent justice:
kenneled life mutinies
nonplusses oppressors' peace
quicksands rank

simian twins understudy
vitriolic wardens
xeroxing you, zookeeper.

ERASERS

Addle brained, clapping dusty erasers

fourth-graders' hopscotch itch
jitters kid limbs. Mrs. Norbert's
ogre presence quickly renders
students tamed
until vigor wilts—xed—
yielding zeros.

CARPE DIEM

Atrophied bones calcified
dust encrusted fragments
give hint, intimate juvenile knack
lusty majesty

Now only pitifully quaint remnants
shrunken telltales
urn varnish
Weariness xes youth's zest

A BLURB COMPENDIUM

"A bubbly collection.... Deft!"
        —Evan Fenton, *Georgetown Herald*

"Inventive joyride."
        —Kenneth Langdon Mays, *Nation*

"Offbeat poems.... Quirky."
        —Rhonda Smollett, *Tikkun*

"Unsurpassed. Very witty."
        —Xavier Yates, *Zuricher*

Maggie Balistreri is a naming consultant and librarian in NYC. Her other books are *The Evasion-English Dictionary* and *There Was a Young Lady Who Swallowed a Lie*.

.

www.ingramcontent.com/pod-product-compliance
Lightning Source LLC
Chambersburg PA
CBHW021123020426
42331CB00004B/612